CGP has Phonics all worked out!

This CGP book is packed with 10-Minute Workouts for Reception Phonics. There are twelve pupil-friendly workouts per term, perfectly matched to the 'Letters and Sounds' programme from the National Curriculum.

They're ideal for on-going assessment, either in the classroom or by parents at home. We've even included progress charts at the back so you can see at a glance how they're getting on.

Published by CGP
ISBN: 978 1 78908 019 3

Written by Karen Bryant-Mole

Editors: Christopher Lindle, Sam Mann, Sam Norman and Jack Tooth

Reviewers: Ross Knaggs, Clare Leck, Lucy Towle

With thanks to Zoe Fenwick, Sharon Gulliver, Anne James and Holly Robinson for the proofreading.

Images throughout the book from www.edu-clips.com

Printed by Elanders Ltd, Newcastle upon Tyne.

Based on the classic CGP style created by Richard Parsons.

Text, design, layout and original illustrations
© Coordination Group Publications Ltd. (CGP) 2018
All rights reserved.

Photocopying this book is not permitted, even if you have a CLA licence.
Extra copies are available from CGP with next day delivery • 0800 1712 712 • www.cgpbooks.co.uk

How to Use this Book

- This book contains 36 workouts. We've split them into 3 sections, one for each term, with 12 workouts each. There's roughly one workout for every week of the school year.

- This book covers Phases 1 to 4 of the Letters & Sounds programme, the Department for Education's systematic synthetic phonics programme. The contents pages will help you identify which part of the Letters & Sounds programme is covered in each workout.

- This book also reinforces the content introduced in CGP's Reception Phonics Targeted Practice Books 1 to 5.

- Each workout is out of 5 marks, shown as stars. Children should shade in the star for each exercise they get right. You can also use the progress charts at the back of the book to track pupils' scores.

Hints for Helpers

Here are a few things to bear in mind when using this book:

- A grey line under two or more letters in a word is a reminder that these letters work together to make one sound. It's a helpful prompt when blending sounds to read words.

- 'Tricky words' are words with letters that have a sound that does not correspond to the expected sound, or that have a sound that has not yet been learned. These words need to be practised until they can be read straight away without blending sounds.

- 'Word frames' are used in spelling and writing activities. The word frames have one box for each sound in the word. The letter or letters for that sound are shown on letter cards. The letters can be copied into the word frame boxes.

- This resource requires children to match images to words. You may need to help children to identify some images they're not sure of.

Contents — Autumn Term

Workout 1 2
- Review Phase 1

Workout 2 4
- Review Phase 1
- Oral blending and segmenting

Workout 3 6
- Phase 2 sounds: s, a, t, p

Workout 4 8
- Phase 2 sounds: i, n, m + review s
- Blending for reading

Workout 5 10
- Phase 2 sound: d + review a, t, p
- Read simple captions

Workout 6 12
- Review Phase 2 sounds: i, n, m, d
- Blending for reading; read a simple caption

Workout 7 14
- Oral blending and segmenting
- Phase 2 sounds: g, o, c + review d
- Blending for reading; read a simple caption

Workout 8 16
- Phase 2 sounds: k, e, + review g, o
- Read a simple caption; write simple words

Workout 9 18
- Phase 2 sounds: u, r + review c, e
- Read **to** and **the**; write simple words

Workout 10 20
- Phase 2 sounds: h, b + review k, u
- Read **no**; write a simple caption

Workout 11 22
- Phase 2 sounds: f, l + review r, h
- Read words with double consonants: ff, ll, ss

Workout 12 24
- Review Phase 2 sounds: b, f, l, p
- Read **I** and **go**; write a simple caption

Contents — Spring Term

Workout 1 26
- Phase 3 sounds: j, v, w + review b
- Review high-frequency words **it**, **is**, **on**, **in**, **to**, **go**

Workout 2 28
- Phase 3 sounds: x, y + review j, v
- Read captions with **he** and **she**; read a sentence with **the**
- Recognise a sentence

Workout 3 30
- Phase 3 sounds: z, qu + review w, d
- Copy **to** and **the**; read a sentence with **no**

Workout 4 32
- Phase 3 digraphs: sh, ch
- Write a sentence with a capital letter and a full stop

Workout 5 34
- Phase 3 digraphs: th, ng
- Read a sentence with **we** and **be**

Workout 6 36
- Letter names
- Read 2-syllable words; read a sentence with **I**

Workout 7 38
- Phase 3 digraphs and trigraphs: ai, ee, igh
- Copy **no**, **go**, **I**; write a sentence with **to**, **go**, **I**

Workout 8 40
- Phase 3 digraphs: oa, oo, ar
- Read a sentence with **me** and **my**

Workout 9 42
- Phase 3 digraphs: or, ur, ow
- Identify a question; read questions with **you**

Workout 10 44
- Phase 3 digraphs and trigraphs: oi, er, air
- Read a caption with **her**; write a sentence with **no**

Workout 11 46
- Phase 3 trigraphs: ure, ear
- Read compound words; read a sentence with **they**, **are**, **all**

Workout 12 48
- Review Phase 3 digraphs
- Write a sentence with **the**; read a sentence with **was**

Contents — Summer Term

Workout 1 50
- CVCC words
- Copy **me**, **we**, **be**, **he**; write **to** and **me**; read **said** and **so**

Workout 2 52
- CCVC words
- Copy **she**, **was**, **you**; write **we** and **be**; read **come**, **have**, **some**

Workout 3 54
- CCVCC and CCCVC words
- Write **he** and **was**; read **like**, **there**, **were**

Workout 4 56
- Words with adjacent consonants and vowel digraphs
- Copy **they**, **are**, **all**; write **she** and **you**; read **little** and **one**

Workout 5 58
- Read 2-syllable words
- Copy **my** and **her**; write **they**, **are**, **all**; read **do** and **what**

Workout 6 60
- Compound words
- Read questions and answers; write **my** and **her**; read **when** and **out**

Workout 7 62
- Review Phase 2 and Phase 3 digraphs: qu, ck, ch, th
- Read and write tricky words and words with adjacent consonants

Workout 8 64
- Review Phase 3 digraphs: sh, ng, ai, oa
- Read and write tricky words and words with adjacent consonants

Workout 9 66
- Review Phase 3 digraphs: ee, oo, ow, oi
- Read and write tricky words and words with adjacent consonants

Workout 10 68
- Review Phase 3 digraphs: ur, or, ar, er
- Read and write tricky words and words with adjacent consonants

Workout 11 70
- Review Phase 3 trigraphs: igh, air, ear, ure
- Read and write tricky words and words with adjacent consonants

Workout 12 72
- Review Phase 2 double consonants: ss, ff, ll, zz
- Read and write tricky words and words with more than one digraph

Autumn Term: Workout 1

Warm Up

1. Which part of your body do you use to hear sounds?
   Circle the correct picture.

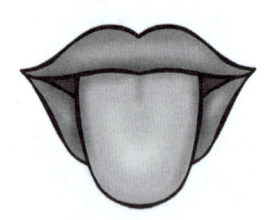

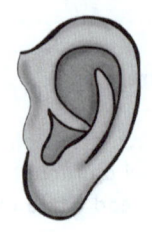

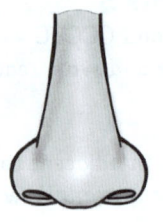

   Which part of your body do you use to taste the food you eat?

   1 star

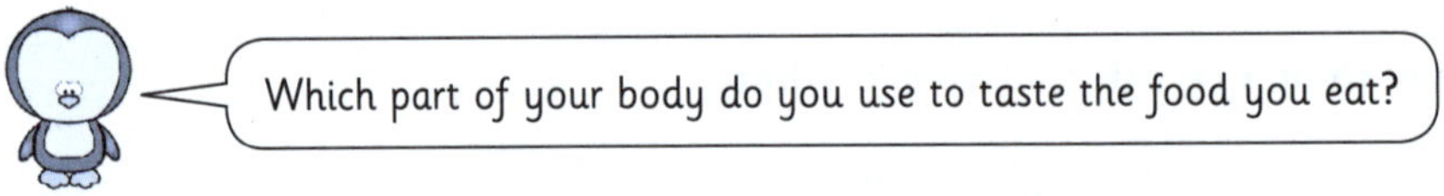

2. **Say** what you see. Each thing makes a different sound.
   If you have heard its sound, **colour** it.

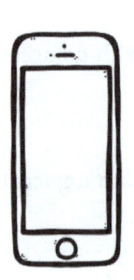

   What's your favourite sound?

   1 star

3. Musical instruments make sounds.
   Circle all the objects that are musical instruments.

   Do you know the names of any musical instruments?

   1 star

4. You can make sounds with your body by clapping and stamping.
   Copy the sound pattern that these children are making.

   CLAP   CLAP   STAMP   CLAP   CLAP   STAMP

   1 star

5. **Colour** the picture of the object that rhymes with the word **shell**.

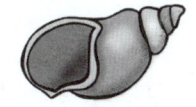

   1 star

   Score   stars

© CGP — not to be photocopied

Autumn Term: Workout 1

Autumn Term: Workout 2

Warm Up

1. **Say** what you see. Two of the words rhyme. One does not.
   Circle the odd one out.

   Can you think of a word that rhymes with frog?

   1 star

2. **Say** what you see. **Think** about the sound it makes.
   Use your voice to make that sound, then **colour** the picture.

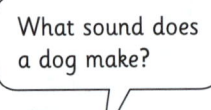

   What sound does a dog make?

   1 star

3. **Say** the sound you hear at the start of **web**.
   Circle the object below that starts with that sound.

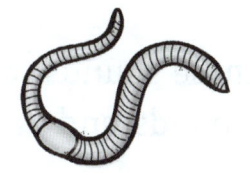

   1 star

4. **Say** what you see. **Say** the sound each word starts with.
   Put a **tick** (✓) below all the things that start with the sound "**r**".

   1 star

5. **Listen** to these sounds: **d - i - sh**.
   Blend the sounds and **say** the word. **Colour** the correct picture.

   What else do you see? Say the word, then say the sounds in the word.

   1 star

   Score   stars

© CGP — not to be photocopied

5

Autumn Term: Workout 2

Autumn Term: Workout 3

Warm Up

1. **Listen** to these sounds: **g - oa - t**.
   Blend the sounds and **say** the word. **Colour** the correct picture.

   What else do you see? Say the word, then say the sounds in the word.

   1 star

2. **Say** what you see. **Say** the sound each word starts with.
   Draw lines to match the objects that start with the same sound.

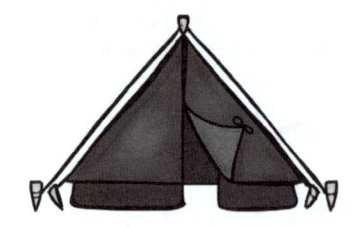

   1 star

3. **Look** at each letter. **Say** its letter sound.
   Match the letter to the object that starts with that sound.

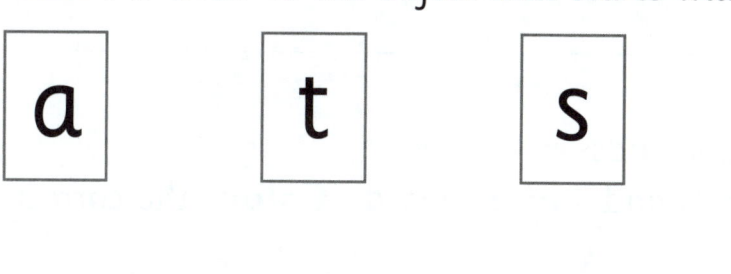

   | a | t | s | p |

   1 star

4. **Write** over the letters. **Start** at the **blue dot**.

   s   a   p   t

   1 star

5. **Name** each object. **Say** the sound it starts with.
   Write the letter for that sound.

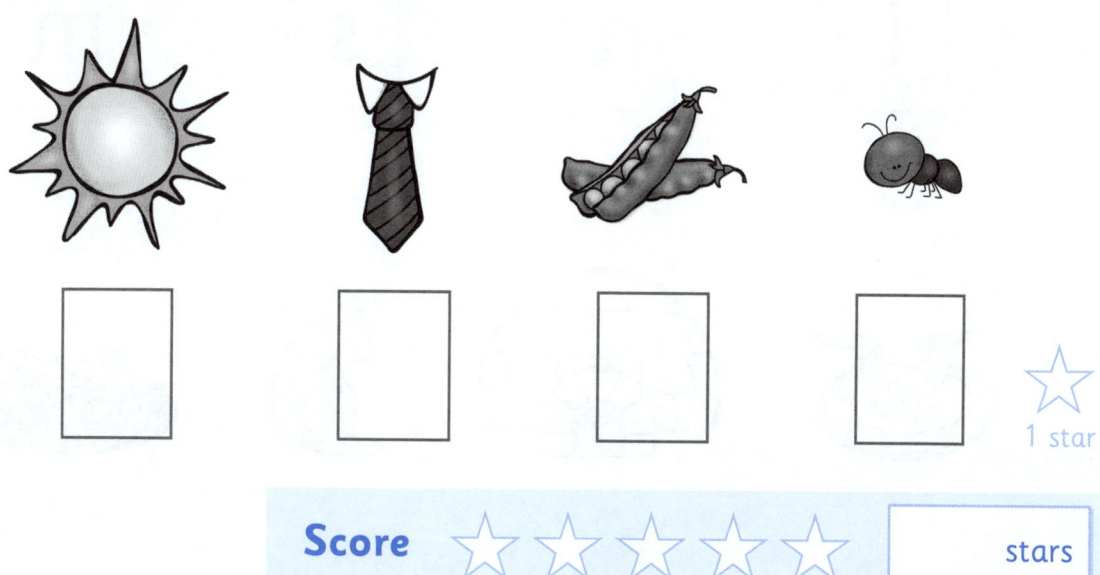

   1 star

   Score ☆☆☆☆☆ stars

   © CGP — not to be photocopied

   Autumn Term: Workout 3

Autumn Term: Workout 4

Warm Up

1. **Listen** to these sounds: **m - u - g**.
   Blend the sounds and **say** the word. **Colour** the correct picture.

   What else do you see? Say the sounds in that word.

   1 star

2. **Look** at each letter. **Say** its letter sound.
   Match the letter to the object that starts with that sound.

   i   n   s   m

   1 star

3. **Write** over the letters. **Start** at the **blue dot**.

s   n   m   i

1 star

4. **Say** what you see. **Say** the sound the word starts with.
   Write the letter for that sound.

1 star

5. **Read** the captions. **Match** each caption to the correct picture.

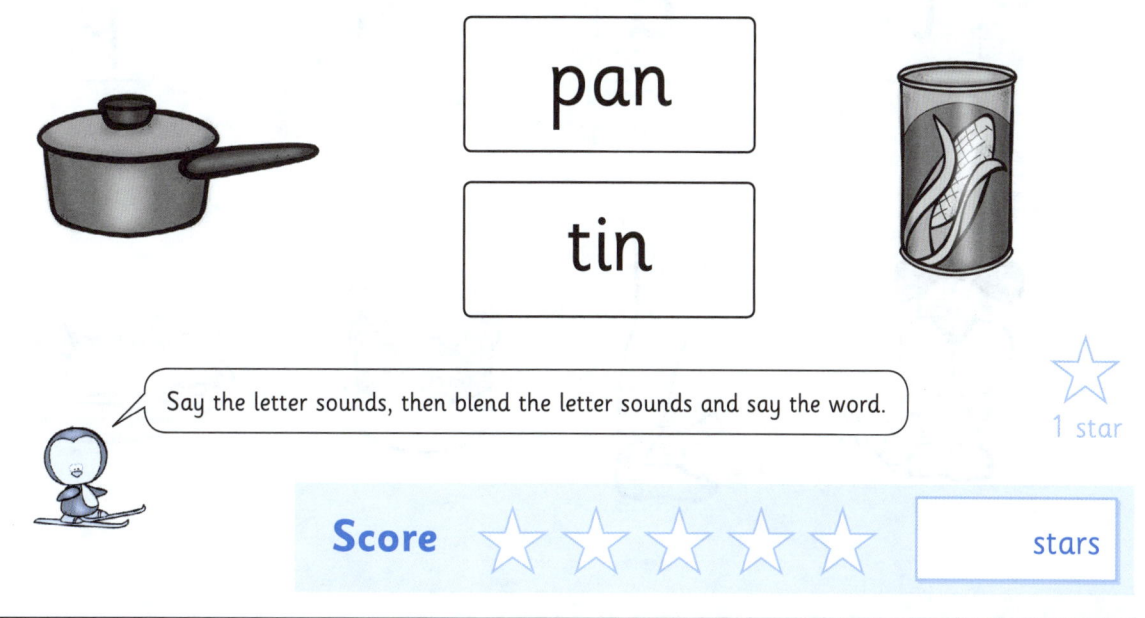

pan

tin

Say the letter sounds, then blend the letter sounds and say the word.

1 star

Score ☆☆☆☆☆ stars

Autumn Term: Workout 4

Autumn Term: Workout 5

Warm Up

1. **Listen** to these sounds: **n - ai - l**.
    Blend the sounds and **say** the word. **Colour** the correct picture.

    Say what else you see. Say the sounds in that word.

    1 star

2. **Look** at each letter. **Say** its letter sound.
    Match the letter to the object that starts with that sound.

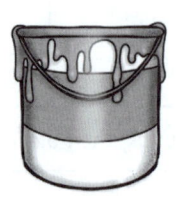

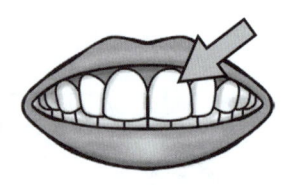

    t   d   a   p

    1 star

3. **Write** over the letters. **Start** at the **blue dot**.

d   t   p   a

☆ 1 star

4. **Say** what you see. **Say** the sound the word starts with. **Write** the letter for that sound.

☆ 1 star

5. **Read** the captions. **Match** each caption to the correct picture.

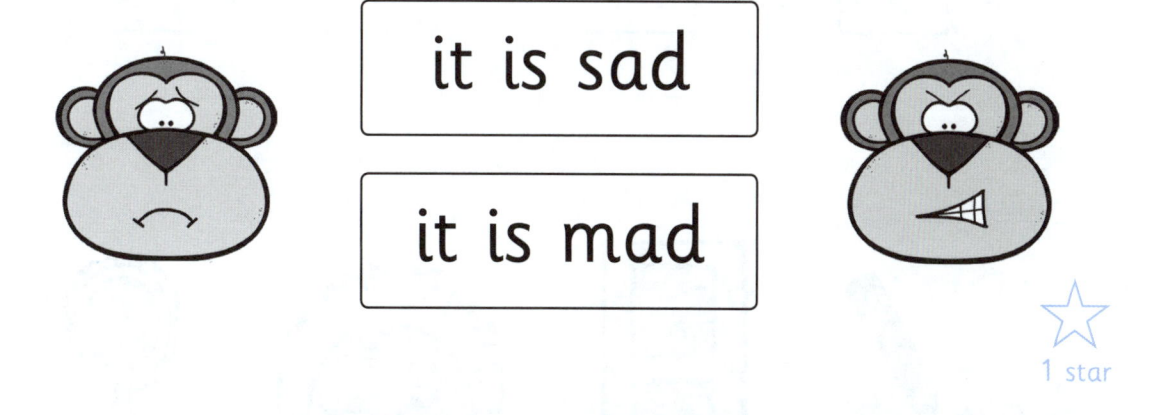

it is sad

it is mad

☆ 1 star

Score ☆☆☆☆☆   stars

Autumn Term: Workout 6

Warm Up

1. **Match** each letter in the top row to its capital in the bottom row.

a m s t n d p i

P T N A M I S D

1 star

2. **Look** at each letter. **Say** its letter sound.
   Match the letter to the object that starts with that sound.

d   m   i   n

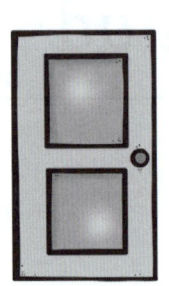

1 star

3. **Write** over the letters. **Start** at the **blue dot**.

i m n d

☆ 1 star

4. **Read** the captions. **Match** each caption to the correct picture.

mat

pad

☆ 1 star

5. **Read** the caption. **Circle** the best picture for the caption.

sit in it

☆ 1 star

Score ☆☆☆☆☆ stars

Autumn Term: Workout 6

Autumn Term: Workout 7

Warm Up

1. **Listen** to these sounds: **t - a - g**.
   Blend the sounds and **say** the word. **Colour** the correct picture.

   1 star

   What else do you see? Say the sounds in that word.

2. **Look** at each letter. **Say** its letter sound.
   Match the letter to the object that starts with that sound.

   c   o   g   d

   1 star

3. **Write** over the letters. **Start** at the **blue dot**.

g o c d

1 star

4. **Read** the captions. **Match** each caption to the correct picture.

cap

cot

1 star

5. **Read** the caption. **Circle** the best picture for the caption.

a man and a dog

1 star

Score ☆☆☆☆☆ stars

Autumn Term: Workout 8

Warm Up

1. **Listen** to these sounds: **f - or - t**.
   Blend the sounds and **say** the word. **Colour** the correct picture.

   Say what else you see. Say the sounds in that word.

   1 star

2. **Look** at each letter in turn. **Say** its letter sound.
   Match the letter to the object that starts with that sound.

   k   e   g   o

   1 star

3. **Write** over the letters. **Start** at the **blue dot**.

o g e k

1 star

4. **Read** the caption. **Circle** the best picture for the caption.

a kid on top

1 star

5. Say **cat** and **peg**. **Say** the sounds in each word.
Write the words in the word frames.

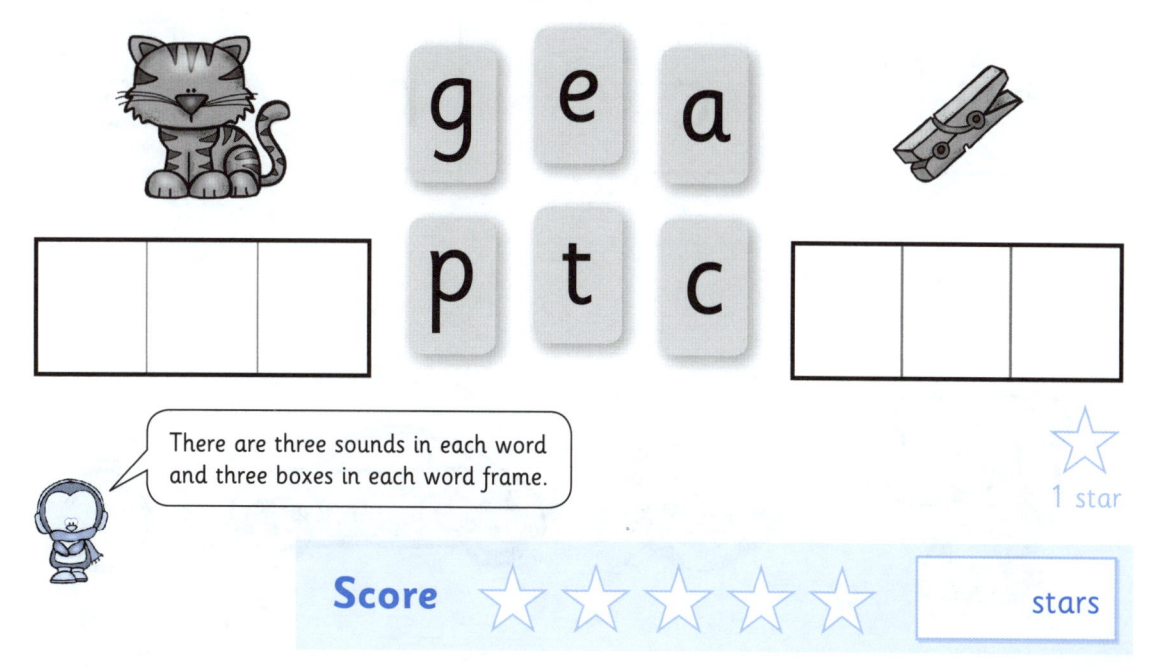

g e a
p t c

There are three sounds in each word and three boxes in each word frame.

1 star

Score ☆☆☆☆☆ stars

Autumn Term: Workout 8

Autumn Term: Workout 9

Warm Up

1. **Listen** to these sounds: l - o - g.
   Blend the sounds and **say** the word. **Colour** the correct picture.

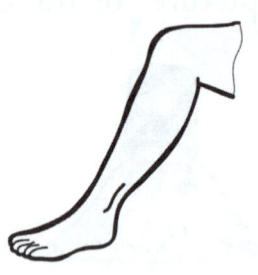

   What else do you see? Say the sounds in that word.

   1 star

2. **Look** at each letter. **Say** its letter sound.
   Match the letter to the object that starts with that sound.

   | u | c | r | e |

   1 star

3. **Write** over the letters. **Start** at the **blue dot**.

e r u c

1 star

4. **Read** the caption. **Circle** the best picture for the caption.

Can you read the tricky words **to** and **the**?

to the rock

1 star

5. Say **sun** and **rod**. **Say** the sounds in each word. **Write** the words in the word frames.

s n
d u
r o

All the letters you need are on the cards!

1 star

Score ☆☆☆☆☆ stars

Autumn Term: Workout 10

Warm Up

1. **Listen** to these sounds: **b - oa - t**.
   Blend the sounds and **say** the word. **Colour** the correct picture.

   Say what else you see. Say the sounds in that word.

   1 star

2. **Look** at each letter. **Say** its letter sound.
   Match the letter to the object that starts with that sound.

   b   k   h   u

   1 star

3. **Write** over the letters. **Start** at the **blue dot**.

h k u b

1 star

4. **Read** the caption. **Circle** the best picture for the caption.

Did you spot the tricky word **no**?

no du<u>ck</u>s on it

1 star

5. Say **a big bus**. **Say** the sounds in each word. **Write** the words in the word frames.

s a i u b b g

1 star

Score ☆☆☆☆☆ stars

Autumn Term: Workout 11

Warm Up

1. **Listen** to these sounds: **b - oo - k**.
   Blend the sounds and **say** the word. **Colour** the correct picture.

   What else do you see? Say the sounds in that word.

   1 star

2. **Look** at each letter. **Say** its letter sound.
   Match the letter to the object that starts with that sound.

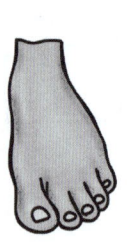

   | f | l | r | h |

   1 star

3. **Write** over the letters. **Start** at the **blue dot**.

r f h l

1 star

4. **Read** the captions. **Match** each caption to the correct picture.

cuff

kiss

1 star

5. **Read** the caption. **Circle** the best picture for the caption.

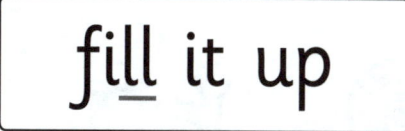

fill it up

1 star

Score ☆☆☆☆☆ stars

Autumn Term: Workout 12

Warm Up

1. **Match** each letter above the dotted line to its capital below the dotted line.

o   g   u   f   c

h   r   e   b   k

....

G   O   K   F   C

H   E   R   U   B

1 star

2. **Look** at each letter. **Say** its letter sound.
   Match the letter to the object that starts with that sound.

p   b   l   f

1 star

3. **Write** over the letters. **Start** at the **blue dot**.

f p b l

1 star

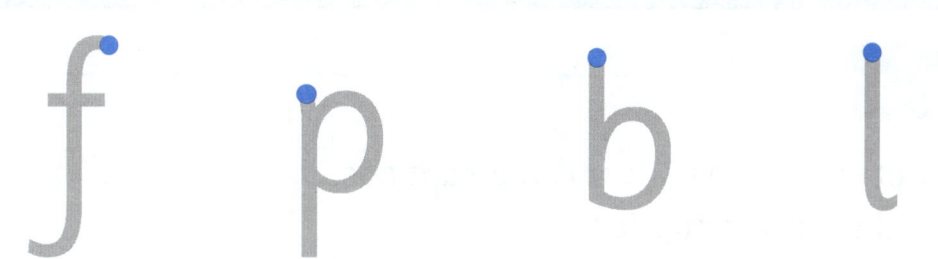

4. **Read** the caption. **Circle** the best picture for the caption.

I and **go** are tricky words.

I let go

1 star

5. Say **a fat pen**. **Say** the sounds in each word. **Write** the words in the word frames.

t f n p e a a

1 star

Score ☆☆☆☆☆ stars

Autumn Term: Workout 12

Spring Term: Workout 1

Warm Up

1. **Look** at the picture. **Read** the captions.
   Circle the correct caption.

   rat

   doll

   1 star

2. **Look** at each letter. **Say** its letter sound.
   Match the letter to the object that starts with that sound.

   w   v   b   j

   1 star

3. **Write** over the letters. **Start** at the **blue dot**.

b   w   j   v

1 star

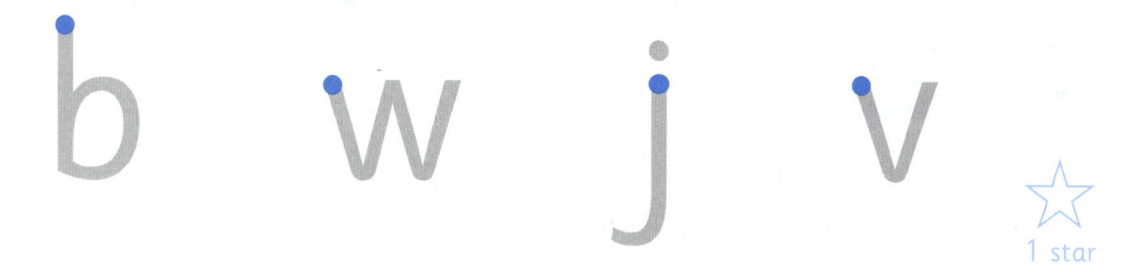

4. **Read** the captions. **Match** each caption to the correct picture.

it is in

it is on

1 star

5. **Read** the caption. **Circle** the best picture for the caption.

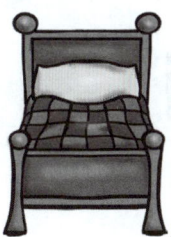

go to bed

1 star

Did you remember the tricky words?

Score ☆☆☆☆☆ stars

Spring Term: Workout 1

Spring Term: Workout 2

Warm Up

1. **Look** at the picture. **Read** the captions.
   Circle the correct caption.

   jug

   web

   1 star

2. **Look** at each letter. **Say** its letter sound.
   Match the letter to the object that starts with that sound.

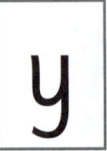

   y   j   v   x

   Look for an object that ends with the sound "**x**".

   1 star

Spring Term: Workout 2 — 28 — © CGP — not to be photocopied

3. **Write** over the letters. **Start** at the **blue dot**.

j   y   x   v

1 star

4. **Read** the captions. **Match** each caption to the correct picture.

he kicks

she kicks

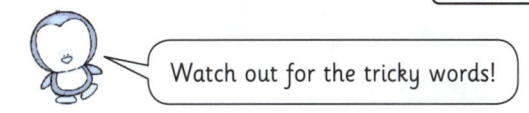

Watch out for the tricky words!

1 star

5. Sentences need to be written in a special way.
   Circle the sentence that is written correctly.

the dog is wet

The dog is wet.

The tricky word **the** looks different with a capital letter.

1 star

Score ☆☆☆☆☆ stars

Spring Term: Workout 2

Spring Term: Workout 3

Warm Up

1. **Look** at the picture. **Read** the captions.
   Circle the correct caption.

   van

   yum

   1 star

2. **Look** at each letter. **Say** its letter sound.
   Match the letter to the object that starts with that sound.

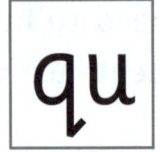

   z   w   d   qu

   There are two letters here. They go together to make the sound "qu".

   1 star

Spring Term: Workout 3   30   © CGP — not to be photocopied

3. **Write** over the letters. **Start** at the **blue dot**.

d   z   w   q

1 star

4. **Read** these tricky words. **Copy** them into the word frames.

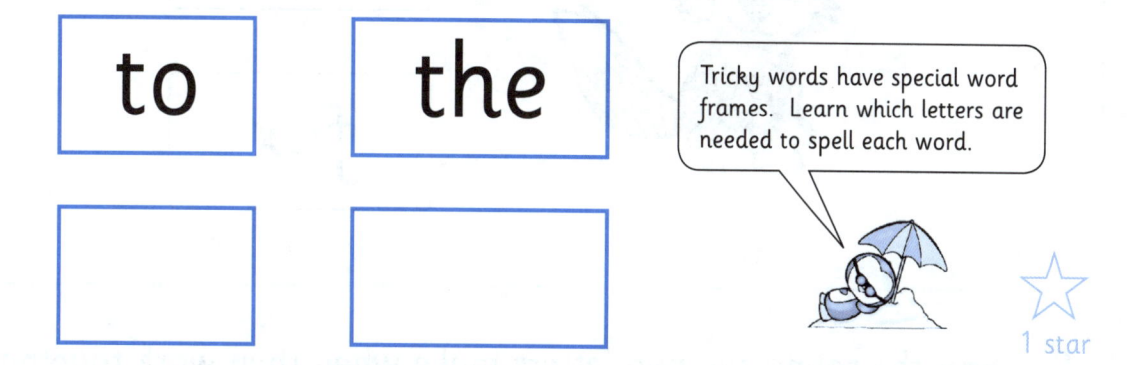

| to | the |

Tricky words have special word frames. Learn which letters are needed to spell each word.

1 star

5. **Read** the sentence. **Circle** the best picture for the sentence.

There's another tricky word in this sentence.

It has no fizz.

1 star

Score ⭐⭐⭐⭐⭐ stars

Spring Term: Workout 3

Spring Term: Workout 4

Warm Up

1. **Look** at the picture. **Read** the captions.
   Circle the correct caption.

   zip

   fox

   1 star

2. **Say** the sound the two letters make when they work together.
   Match the letters to the objects that start with that sound.

   sh   ch

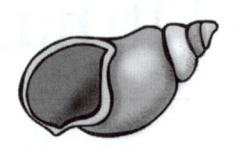

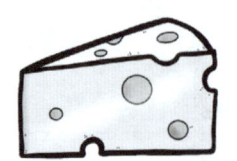

   1 star

3. **Read** the captions. **Match** each caption to the correct picture.

ship

chick

1 star

4. **Look** at the picture. **Write** the letters that complete the word.

o p   sh   ch

Remember. The two letters go in one box because they make one sound.

1 star

5. **Say** this sentence: **Mud is fun.** **Write** the sentence.

d   M   s   .   f

i   u   n   u

Sentences need a capital letter at the start and a full stop at the end.

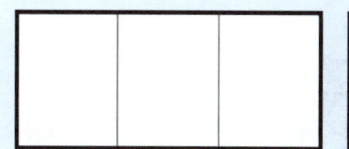

1 star

Score ☆☆☆☆☆ stars

© CGP — not to be photocopied

33

Spring Term: Workout 4

Spring Term: Workout 5

Warm Up

1. **Look** at the picture. **Read** the captions.
   Circle the caption that tells you the sound the animal makes.

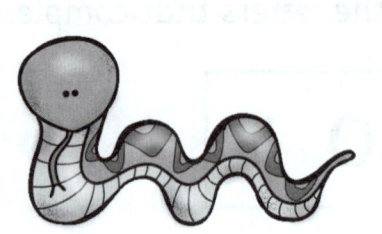

   hiss

   quack

   1 star

2. **Say** the sound the two letters make when they work together.
   Match the letters to the objects that end with that sound.

   th   ng

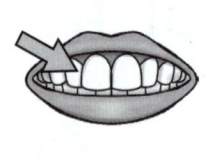

   1 star

Spring Term: Workout 5   34   © CGP — not to be photocopied

3. **Read** the captions. **Match** each caption to the correct picture.

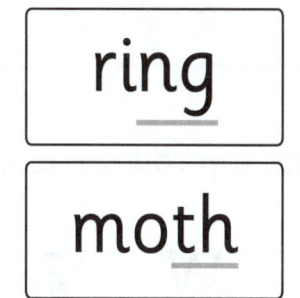

ring

moth

1 star

4. **Look** at the picture. **Write** the letters that complete the word.

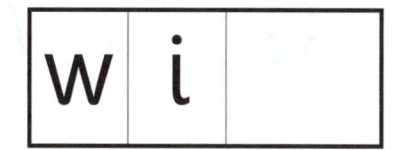

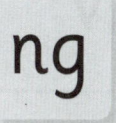

w | i |

th   ng

1 star

5. **Read** the sentence. **Circle** the best picture for the sentence.

We will be rich.

Did you spot the tricky words in this sentence?

1 star

Score ☆☆☆☆☆   stars

© CGP — not to be photocopied

35

Spring Term: Workout 5

Spring Term: Workout 6

Warm Up

1. **Match** each letter in the top row to its capital in the bottom row.

y   x   v   w   z   j   q

V   Z   Y   Q   X   W   J

1 star

2. Letters have names as well as sounds. **Say** the name of each letter. Put a **tick** (✓) below each letter name you know.

a   b   c   d   e   f   g   h   i
☐   ☐   ☐   ☐   ☐   ☐   ☐   ☐   ☐

j   k   l   m   n   o   p   q   r
☐   ☐   ☐   ☐   ☐   ☐   ☐   ☐   ☐

s   t   u   v   w   x   y   z
☐   ☐   ☐   ☐   ☐   ☐   ☐   ☐

1 star

3. **Read** the captions. **Match** each caption to the correct picture.

bucket

rubbish

1 star

4. **Look** at the picture. **Write** the word.

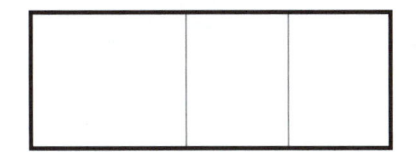

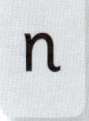

n   i   ch

The letters you need are on the cards.

1 star

5. **Read** the sentence. **Circle** the best picture for the sentence.

There's another tricky word here. It appears twice!

I wish I had a rabbit.

1 star

Score   stars

Spring Term: Workout 6

Spring Term: Workout 7

Warm Up

1. **Draw** over the dots to write the capital letters. **Start** at the **blue dot**.

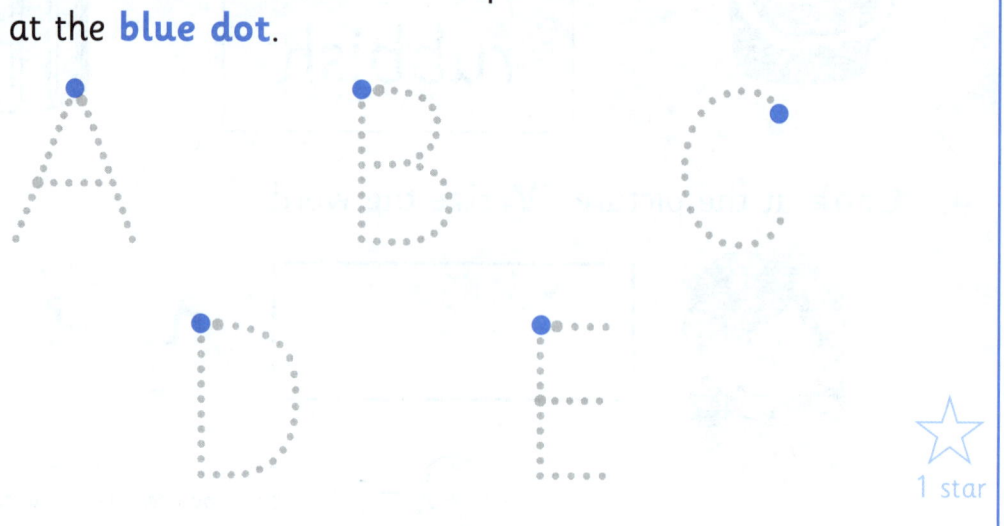

   A B C

   D E

   1 star

2. **Say** the sound these letters make when they work together. **Match** them to an object that has that sound in it.

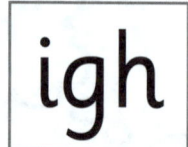

   ai   ee   igh

   1 star

3. **Look** at the picture. **Circle** the best caption.

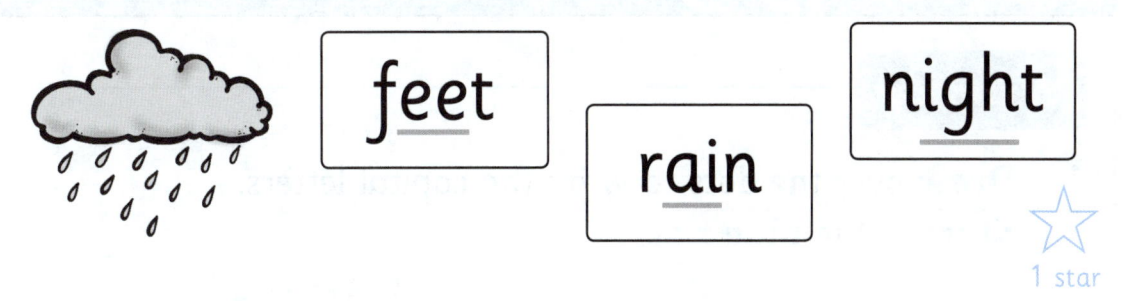

feet   rain   night

1 star

4. **Read** these tricky words. **Copy** them into the word frames.

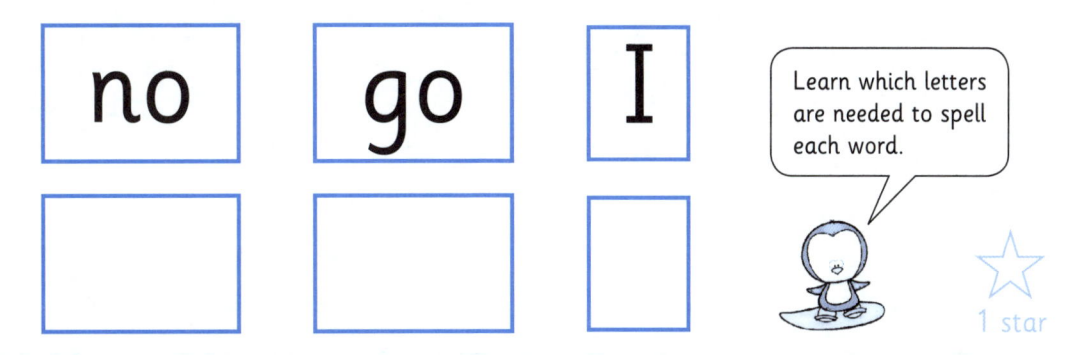

no   go   I

Learn which letters are needed to spell each word.

1 star

5. **Say** this sentence: **I go to jail.** **Write** the sentence.

l   j   ai   .

There are no letter cards for the tricky words **I**, **go** and **to**. You know how to spell these!

1 star

Score ☆☆☆☆☆ stars

Spring Term: Workout 7

Spring Term: Workout 8

Warm Up

1. **Draw** over the dots to write the capital letters. **Start** at the **blue dot**.

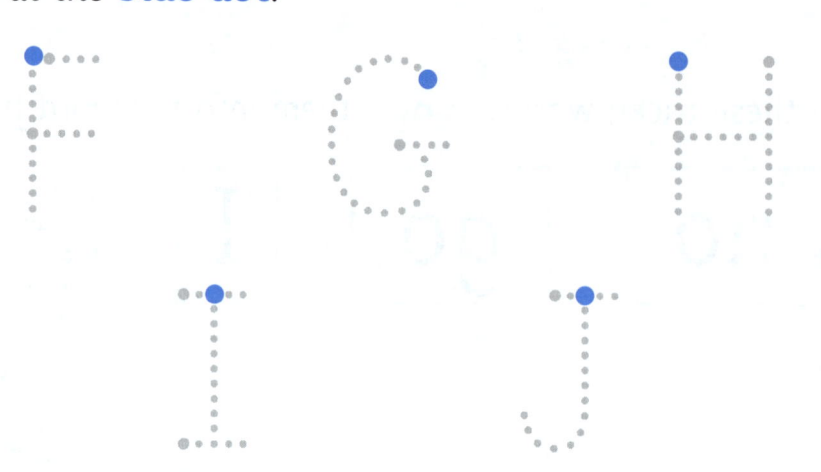

   F G H

   I J

   1 star

2. **Say** the sound these letters make when they work together. **Match** them to an object that has that sound in it.

   | oa | oo | ar |

   1 star

3. **Look** at the picture. **Circle** the best caption.

cart   boot   coat

1 star

4. **Read** the captions. **Match** each caption to the correct picture.

in the car

on the boat

1 star

5. **Read** the sentence. **Circle** the best picture for the sentence.

Look at me. My jeep is cool.

1 star

Did you spot two tricky words?

Score ☆☆☆☆☆ stars

Spring Term: Workout 9

Warm Up

1. **Draw** over the dots to write the capital letters.
   Start at the **blue dot**.

   K   L   M
   N   O

   1 star

2. **Say** the sound these letters make when they work together.
   Match them to an object that has that sound in it.

   or   ur   ow

   1 star

3. **Look** at the picture. **Circle** the best caption.

| cow | fur | horn |

1 star

4. **Read** the sentences.
   Put a **tick** (✓) next to the sentence that is question.

Is this a torch? ☐

This is a torch. ☐

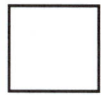

1 star

5. **Read** the question. **Circle** the answer that is true for you.

Can you bow?   yes / no

Can you surf? yes / no

1 star

Score ☆☆☆☆☆ stars

Spring Term: Workout 9

Spring Term: Workout 10

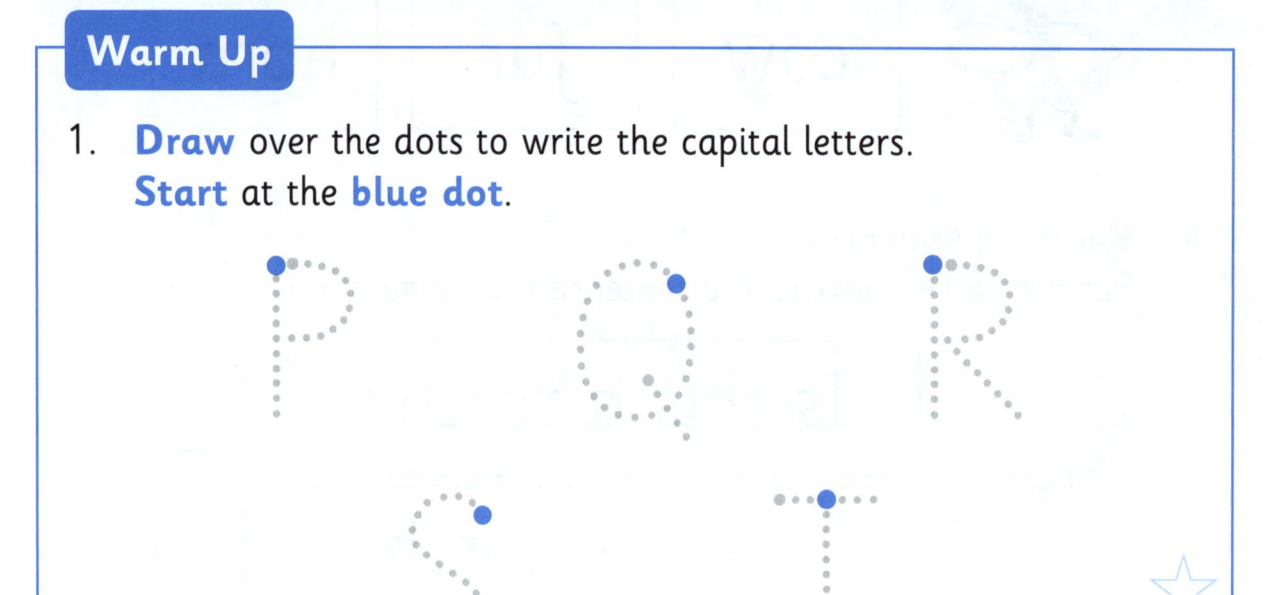

Warm Up

1. **Draw** over the dots to write the capital letters.
   Start at the **blue dot**.

   P Q R
   S T

   1 star

2. **Say** the sound these letters make when they work together.
   Match them to an object that has that sound in it.

   | oi | er | air |

   1 star

3. **Look** at the picture. **Circle** the best caption.

| foil | hair | river |

1 star

4. **Read** the captions. **Match** each caption to the correct picture.

| her dinner |
| his dinner |

1 star

5. **Say** this sentence: **It had no oil.** **Write** the sentence.

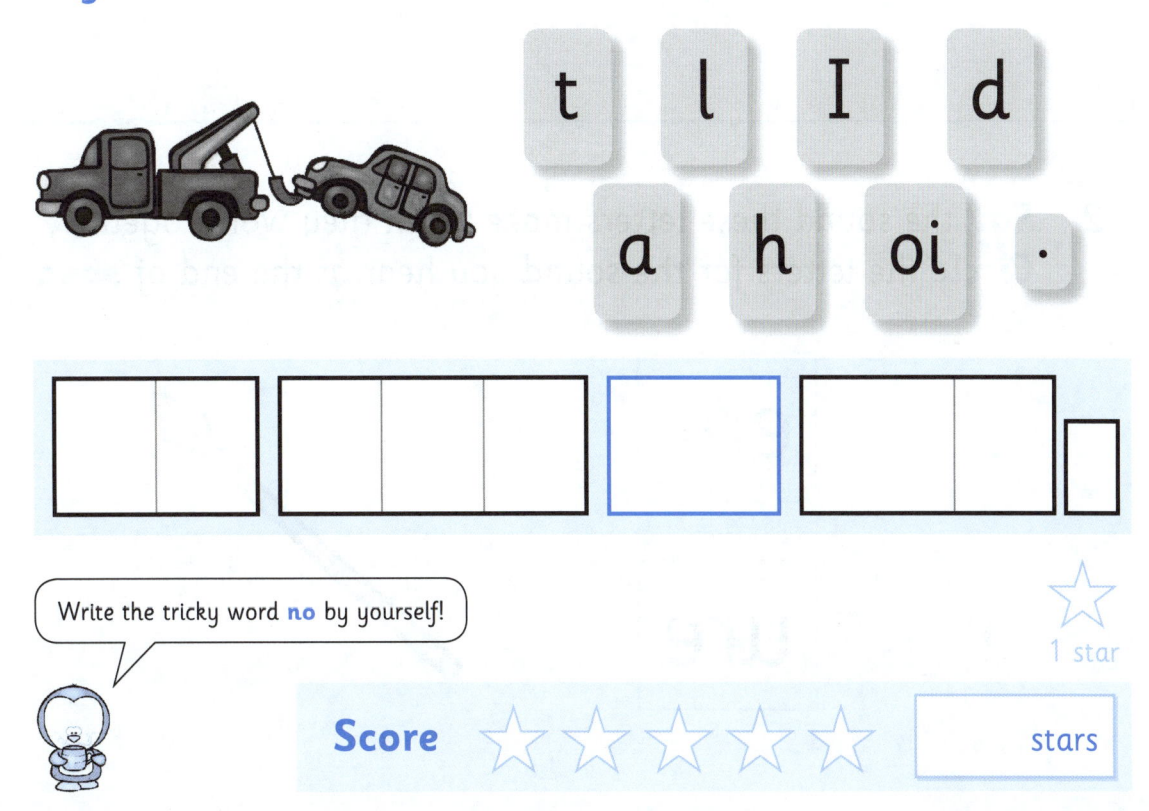

t l I d

a h oi .

Write the tricky word **no** by yourself!

1 star

Score ☆☆☆☆☆   stars

Spring Term: Workout 11

Warm Up

1. **Draw** over the dots to write the capital letters. **Start** at the **blue dot**.

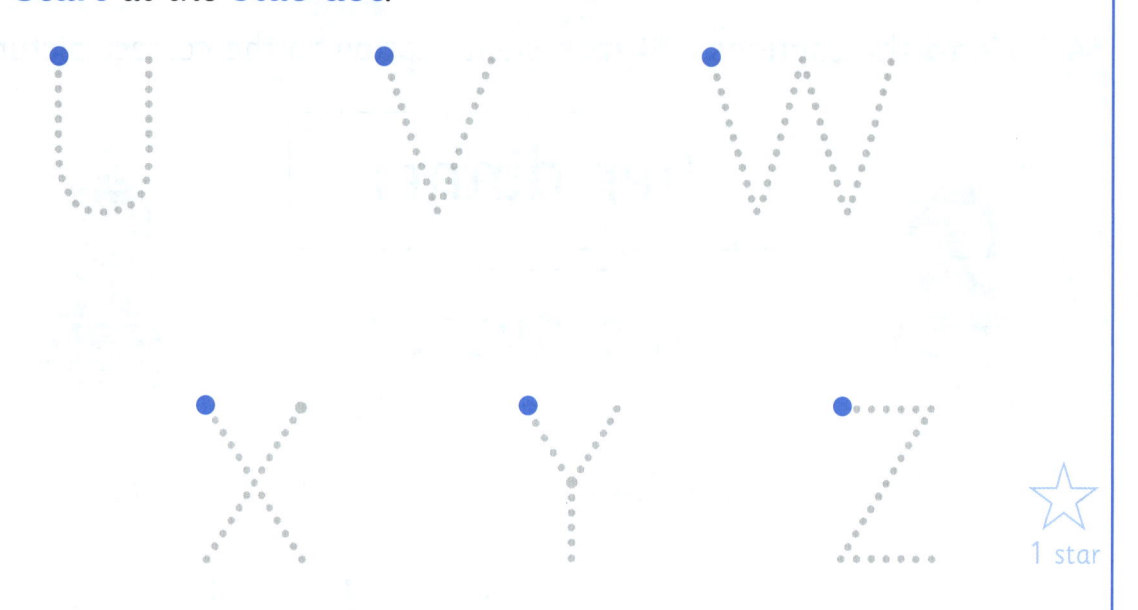

   U V W

   X Y Z

   1 star

2. **Say** the sound these letters make when they work together. **Circle** the letters for the sound you hear at the end of **spear**.

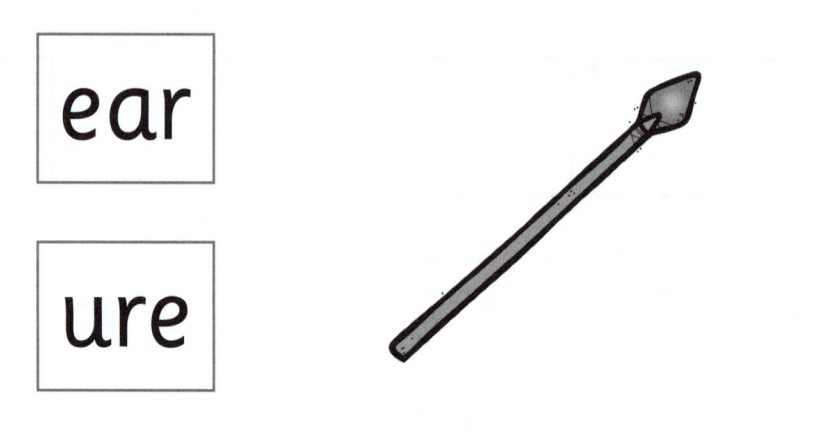

   ear

   ure

   1 star

3. **Look** at the picture. **Circle** the best caption.

cure   hear

1 star

4. **Read** the captions. **Match** each caption to the correct picture.

backpack

sunset

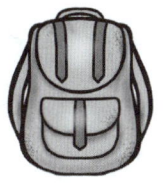

1 star

5. **Read** the sentence. **Circle** the best picture for the sentence.

They are all in tears.

1 star

Did you spot three tricky words?

Score ☆☆☆☆☆ stars

Spring Term: Workout 12

Warm Up

1. **Say** what you see.
   Circle the letters for the sound the word ends with.

   ch   sh

   ng   th

   1 star

2. **Say** the sound these letters make when they work together.
   Match them to an object that has that sound in it.

   or   ow   ai   ar

   1 star

3. **Look** at the picture. **Circle** the best caption.

curl   soap   soil

1 star

4. **Say** this sentence: **I see the zoo.** **Write** the sentence.

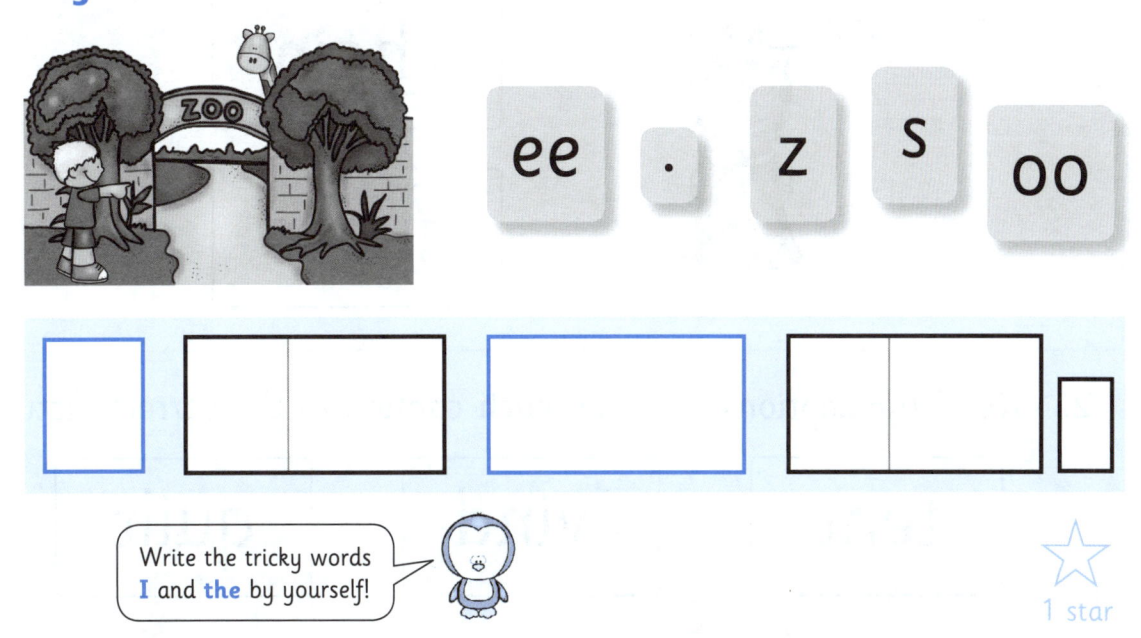

ee . z s oo

Write the tricky words **I** and **the** by yourself!

1 star

5. **Read** the sentence. **Circle** the best picture for the sentence.

Up high the air was pure.

Just two tricky words this time!

1 star

Score   stars

Spring Term: Workout 12

Summer Term: Workout 1

Warm Up

1. **Look** at the picture. **Read** the captions.
   Circle the correct caption.

   chain

   queen

   1 star

2. **Read** the captions. **Match** each caption to the correct picture.

   tent   wind   quilt

   1 star

3. **Read** these tricky words. **Copy** them into the word frames.

   me   we   be   he

   1 star

4. Say this sentence: **Kick it to me.** **Write** the sentence.

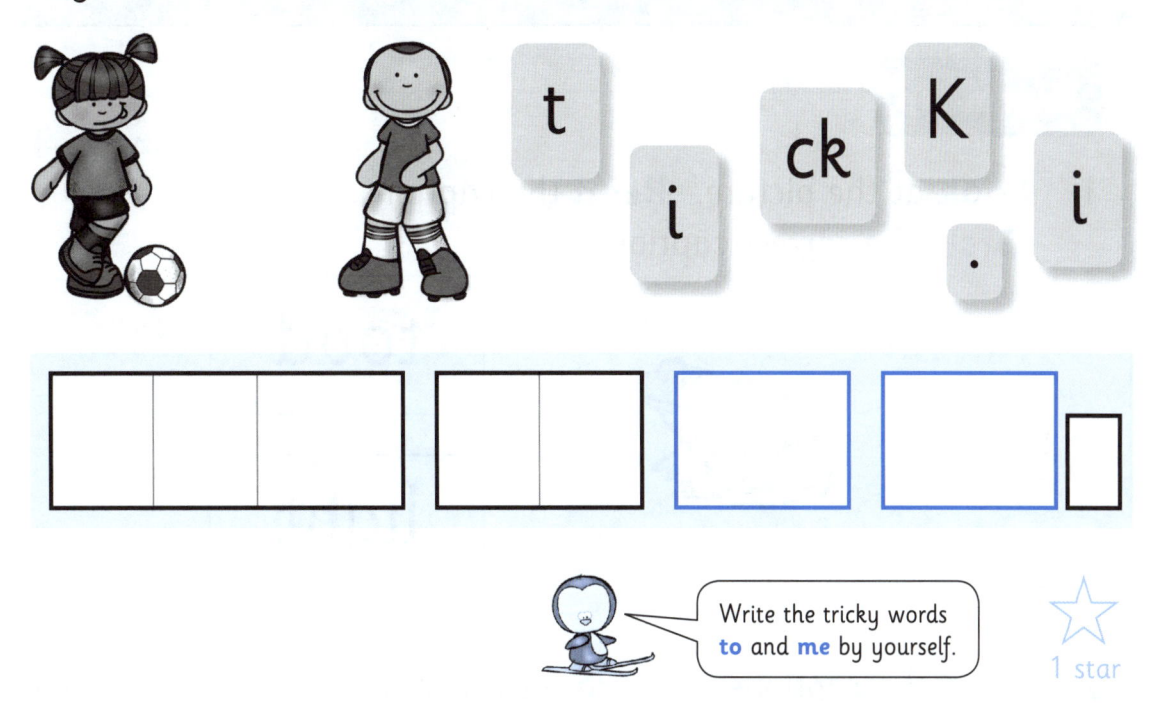

Write the tricky words **to** *and* **me** *by yourself.*

1 star

5. **Read** the sentence. **Circle** the best picture for the sentence.

She said it felt so soft.

1 star

Score ☆☆☆☆☆ stars

Summer Term: Workout 2

Warm Up

1. **Look** at the picture. **Read** the captions.
   Circle the correct caption.

   toad

   light

   1 star

2. **Read** the captions. **Match** each caption to the correct picture.

   pram   crash   flag

   1 star

3. **Read** these tricky words. **Copy** them into the word frames.

   she   was   you

   1 star

4. Say this sentence: **We will be fit.** **Write** the sentence.

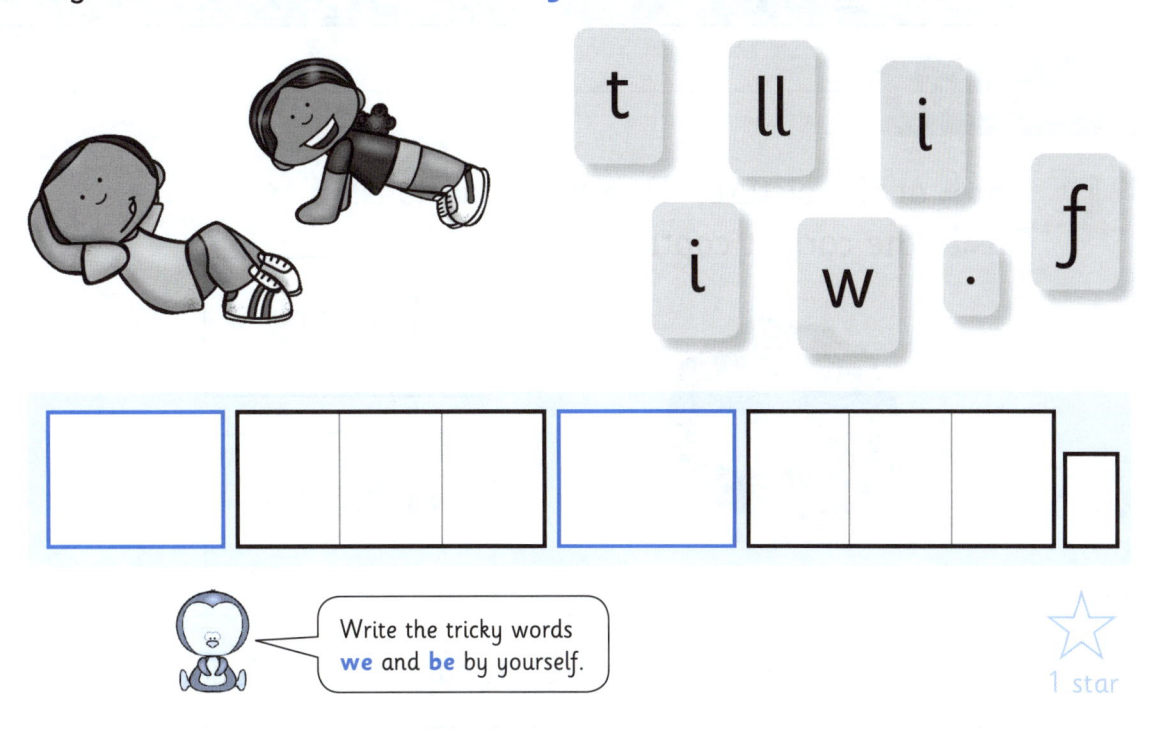

Write the tricky words **we** and **be** by yourself.

1 star

5. **Read** the sentence. **Circle** the best picture for the sentence.

Come and have some snacks.

1 star

Score ☆☆☆☆☆ stars

© CGP — not to be photocopied

53

Summer Term: Workout 2

Summer Term: Workout 3

Warm Up

1. **Look** at the picture. **Read** the captions.
   Circle the correct caption.

   burn

   beard

   1 star

2. **Read** the captions. **Match** each caption to the correct picture.

   slept   swept   drank

   1 star

3. **Look** at the picture. **Read** the sentences.
   Circle the best sentence.

   I like snipping.

   I like sticking.

   1 star

4. Say this sentence: **He was wet.** **Write** the sentence.

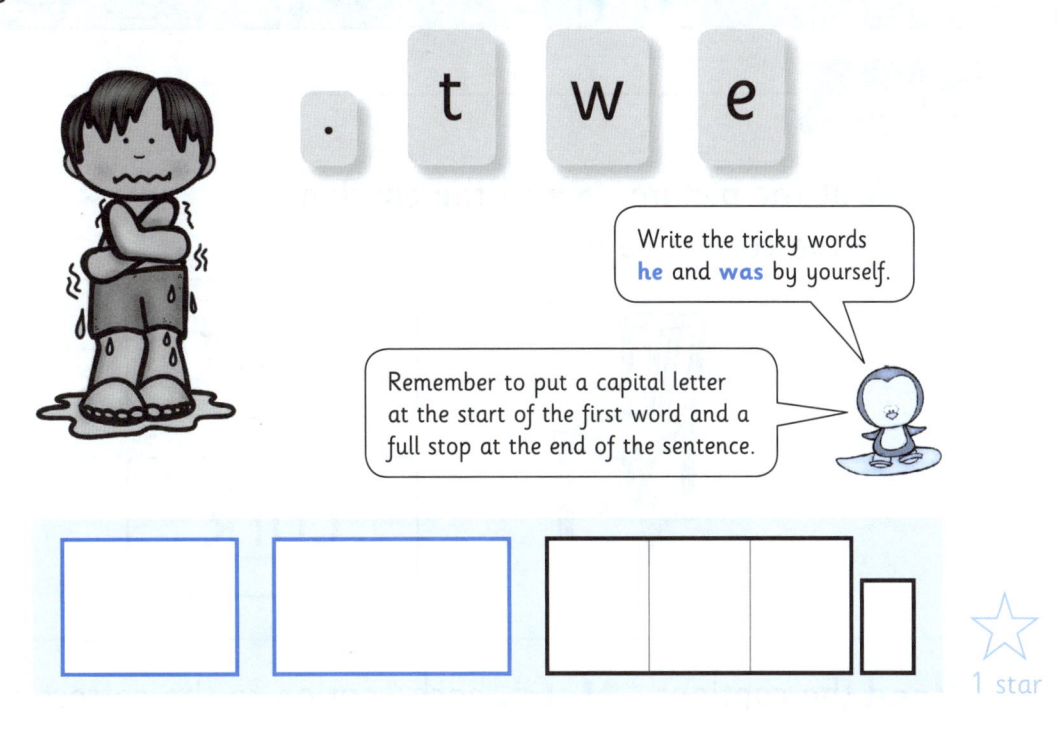

 . t w e

Write the tricky words **he** and **was** by yourself.

Remember to put a capital letter at the start of the first word and a full stop at the end of the sentence.

1 star

5. **Read** the sentence. **Circle** the best picture for the sentence.

There were lots of scraps.

1 star

Score stars

Summer Term: Workout 4

Warm Up

1. **Look** at the picture. **Read** the captions.
   Circle the correct caption.

   chair

   cork

   1 star

2. **Read** the captions. **Match** each caption to the correct picture.

   storm   crown   train

   1 star

3. **Read** these tricky words. **Copy** them into the word frames.

   they   all   are

   1 star

4. Say this sentence: **She picks you.** **Write** the sentence.

Write the tricky words **she** and **you** by yourself.

1 star

5. **Read** the sentence. **Circle** the best picture for the sentence.

The little one looks sweet.

1 star

Score ☆☆☆☆☆ stars

Summer Term: Workout 5

Warm Up

1. **Look** at the picture. **Read** the captions.
   Circle the correct caption.

   town

   farm

   1 star

2. **Read** the captions. **Match** each caption to the correct picture.

   igloo   mushroom   balloon

   1 star

3. **Read** these tricky words. **Copy** them into the word frames.

   my   her

   Remember that you need to learn which letters are needed to spell tricky words.

   1 star

4. Say this sentence: **They are all long.** **Write** the sentence.

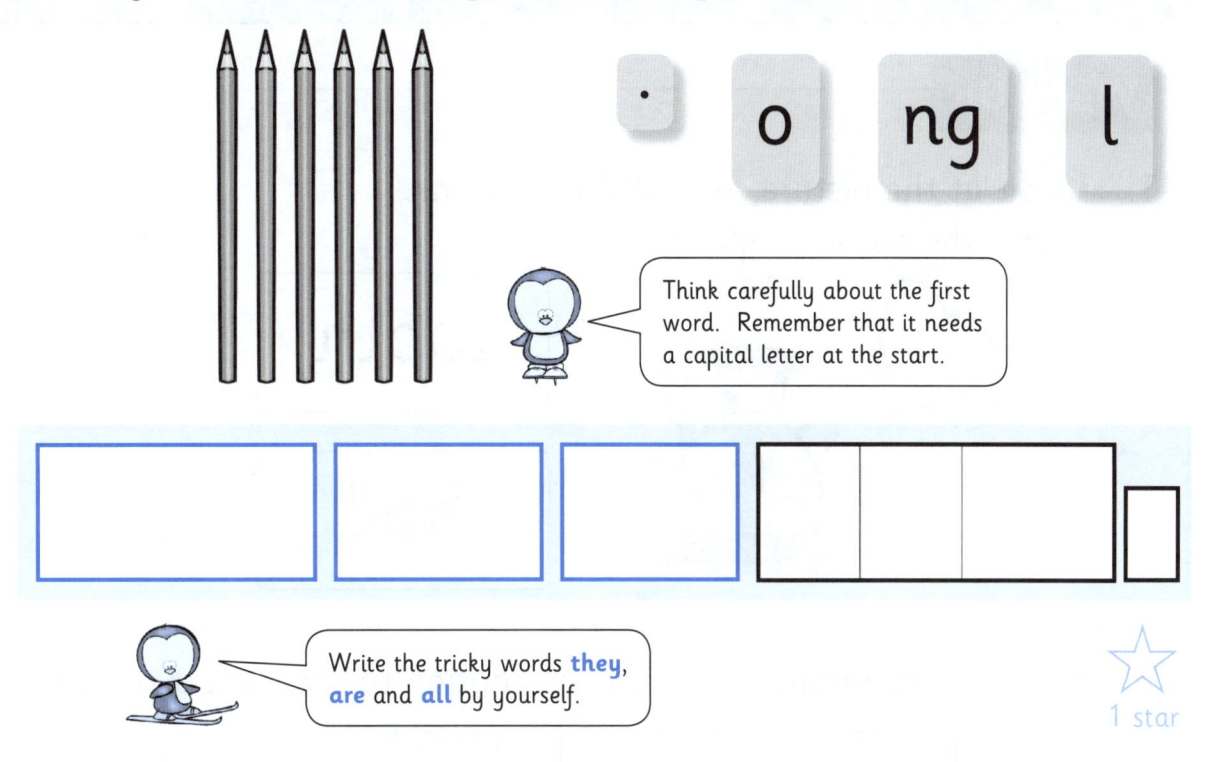

Think carefully about the first word. Remember that it needs a capital letter at the start.

Write the tricky words **they**, **are** and **all** by yourself.

1 star

5. **Read** the sentence. **Circle** the best picture for the sentence.

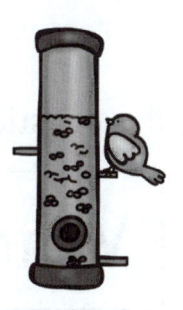

Do what I tell you.

1 star

Score   stars

Summer Term: Workout 6

Warm Up

1. **Look** at the picture. **Read** the captions.
   Circle the correct caption.

   tooth

   boil

   1 star

2. **Read** the captions. **Match** each caption to the correct picture.

   hairbrush

   dustbin

   1 star

3. **Read** the question. **Circle** the correct answer.

   What is a hut?

   a shelter

   a toaster

   1 star

4. Say this sentence: **My mum fed her.** **Write** the sentence.

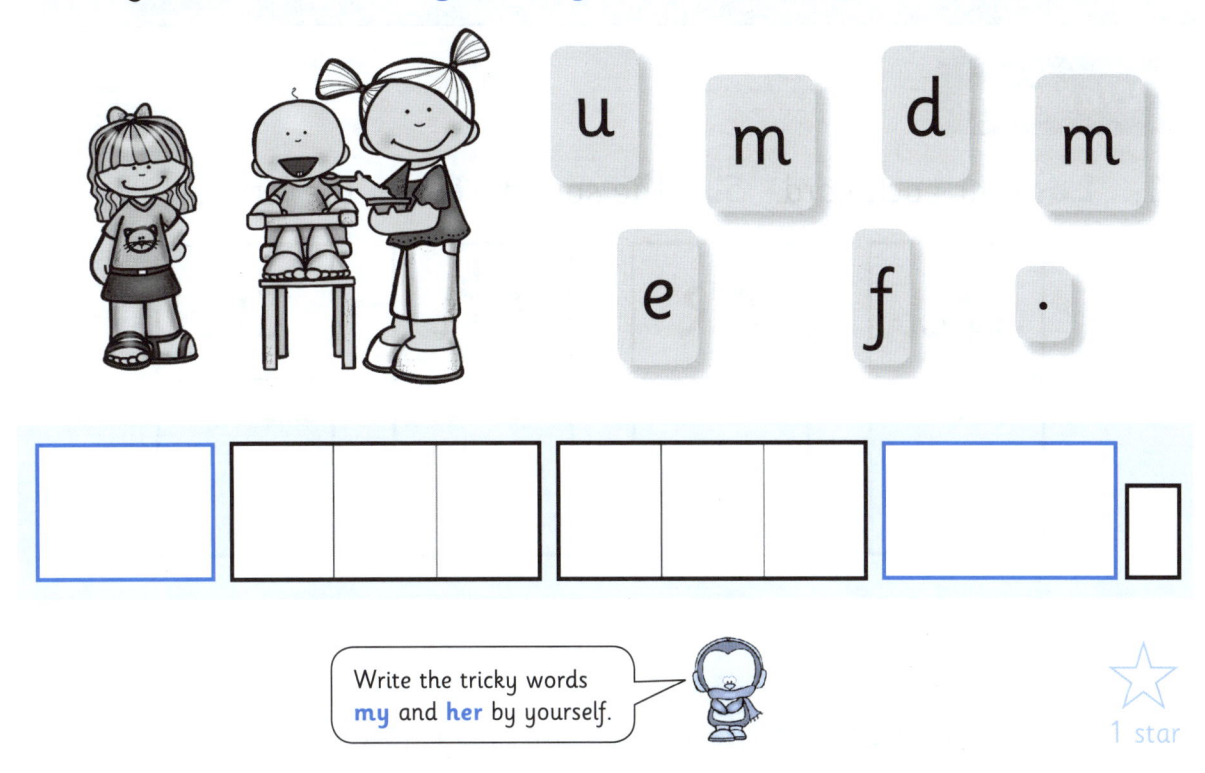

Write the tricky words **my** and **her** by yourself.

1 star

5. **Read** the sentence. **Circle** the best picture for the sentence.

He wept when his mum went out.

1 star

Score   stars

Summer Term: Workout 7

Warm Up

1. **Look** at each card. **Say** the sound. **Copy** the letters.

| qu | ck | ch | th |

1 star

2. **Say** the words **quilt**, **sack**, **chop** and **moth**.
   Write the words in the word frames by yourself.

Say the sounds in each word. Write the letters.

If the sound has two letters, write them both in the same box.

1 star

3. **Look** at the picture. **Read** the captions.
   Circle the best caption for the picture.

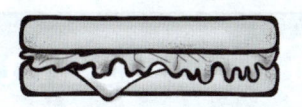

   a black liquid

   a thin sandwich

   You don't need lines under the letters that work together because you've just practised them.

   1 star

4. **Read** the tricky words on the flags.
   Circle the flag if you can read the word straight away.

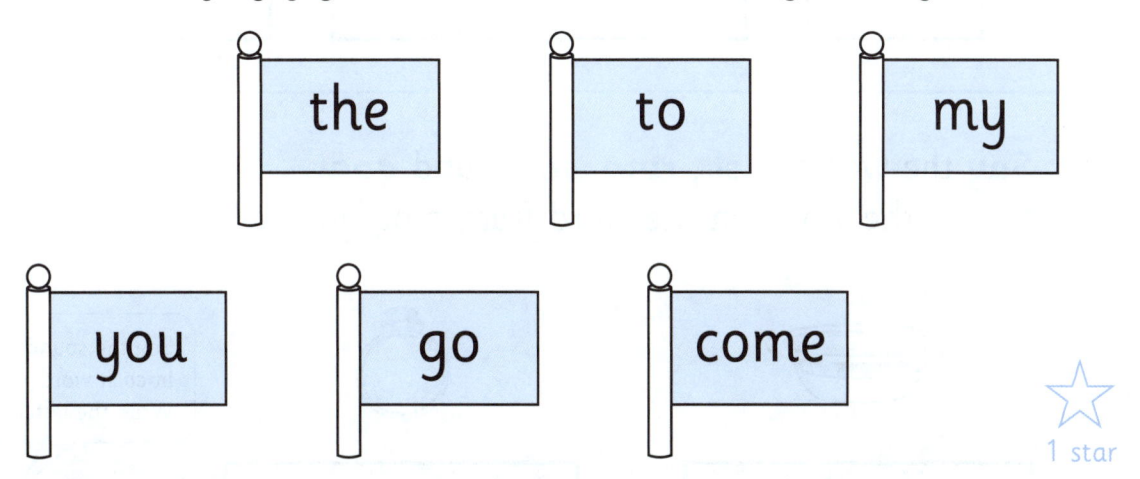

   the   to   my

   you   go   come

   1 star

5. The penguin is saying some common words.
   Listen to the words. **Write** one word on each iceberg.

   in, it, on, at

   1 star

   Score   stars

Summer Term: Workout 8

Warm Up

1. **Look** at each card. **Say** the sound. **Copy** the letters.

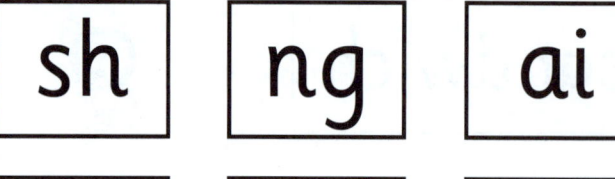

   | sh | ng | ai | oa |

   1 star

2. **Say** the words **dish**, **ring**, **snail** and **goat**.
   Write the words in the word frames by yourself.

   Say the sounds in each word. Write the letters.

   You practised the sounds with two letters in the Warm Up.

   1 star

Summer Term: Workout 8

64

© CGP — not to be photocopied

3. **Look** at the picture. **Read** the captions.
   Circle the best caption for the picture.

   a train and a boat

   a king and a fish

   1 star

4. **Read** the tricky words on the flags.
   Circle the flag if you can read the word straight away.

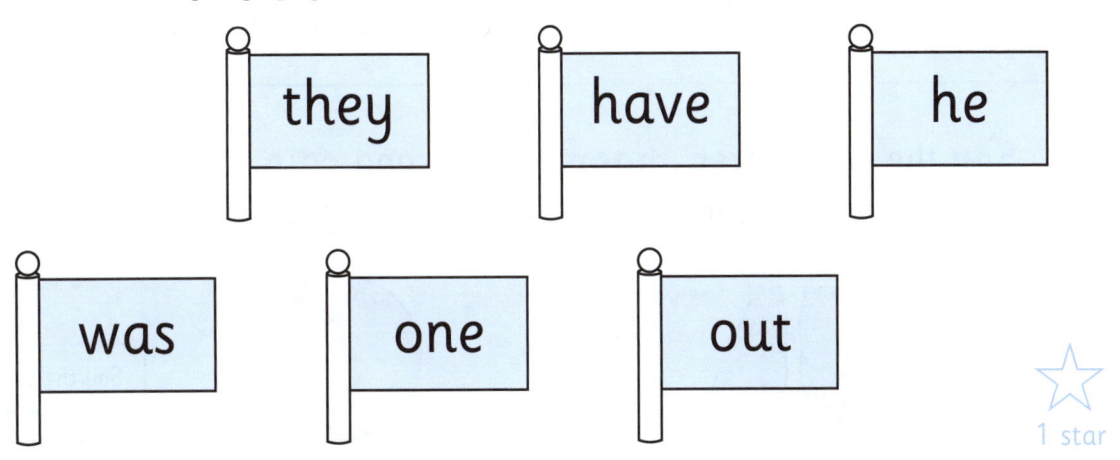

   they   have   he

   was   one   out

   1 star

5. The penguin is doing a trick and saying some tricky words.
   Listen to the tricky words. **Write** one word on each iceberg.

   the, to, go

   1 star

   Score   stars

Summer Term: Workout 8

Summer Term: Workout 9

Warm Up

1. **Look** at each card. **Say** the sound. **Copy** the letters.

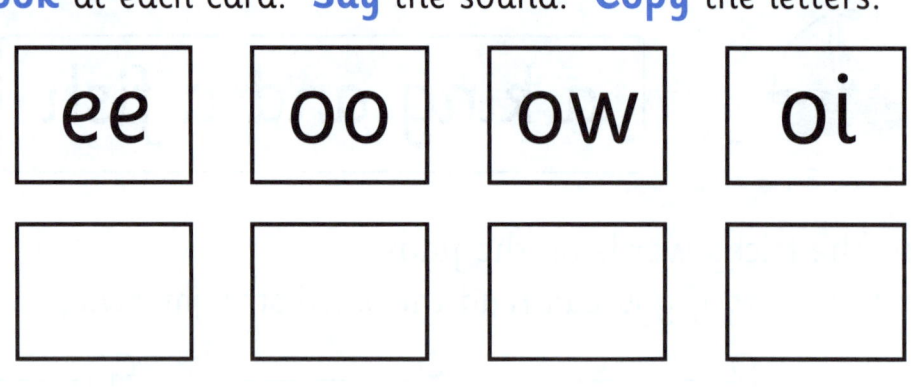

   | ee | oo | ow | oi |

   1 star

2. **Say** the words **feet**, **moon**, **clown** and **coin**.
   Write the words in the word frames by yourself.

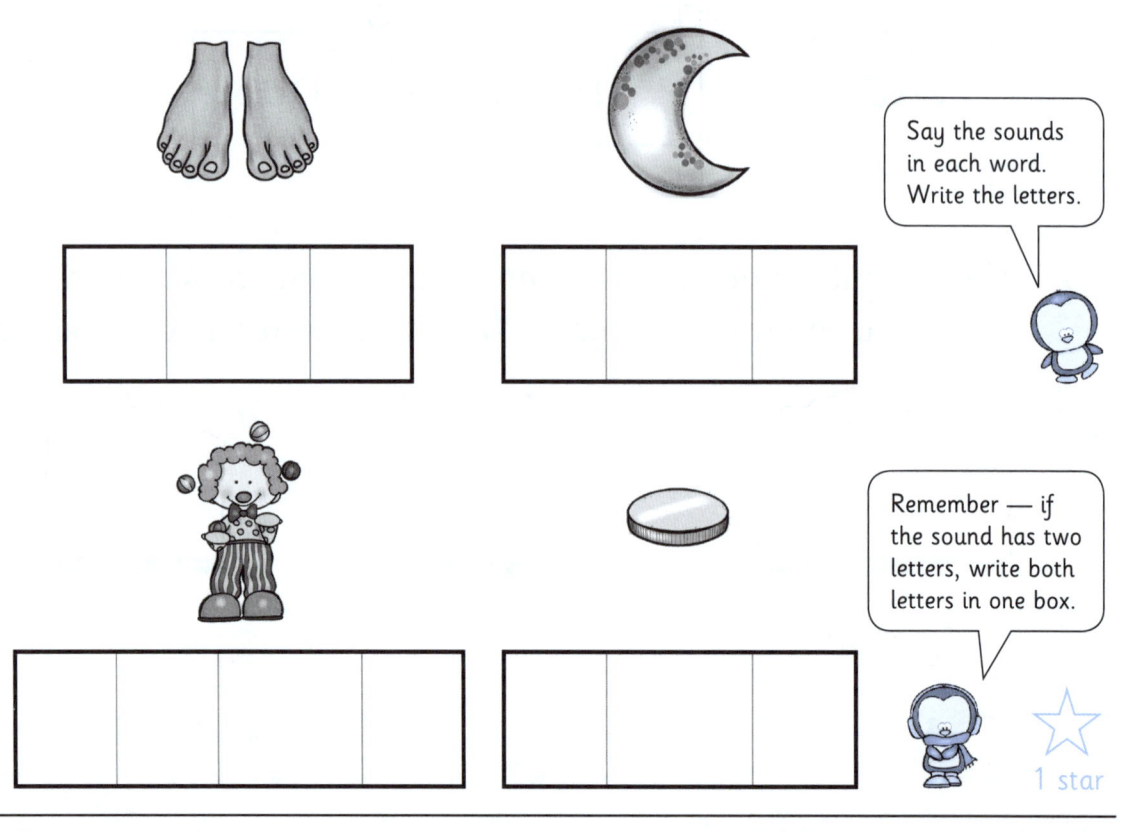

   Say the sounds in each word. Write the letters.

   Remember — if the sound has two letters, write both letters in one box.

   1 star

Summer Term: Workout 9   66   © CGP — not to be photocopied

3. **Look** at the picture. **Read** the captions.
   Circle the best caption for the picture.

   point at an owl

   asleep on a roof

   1 star

4. **Read** the tricky words on the flags.
   Circle the flag if you can read the word straight away.

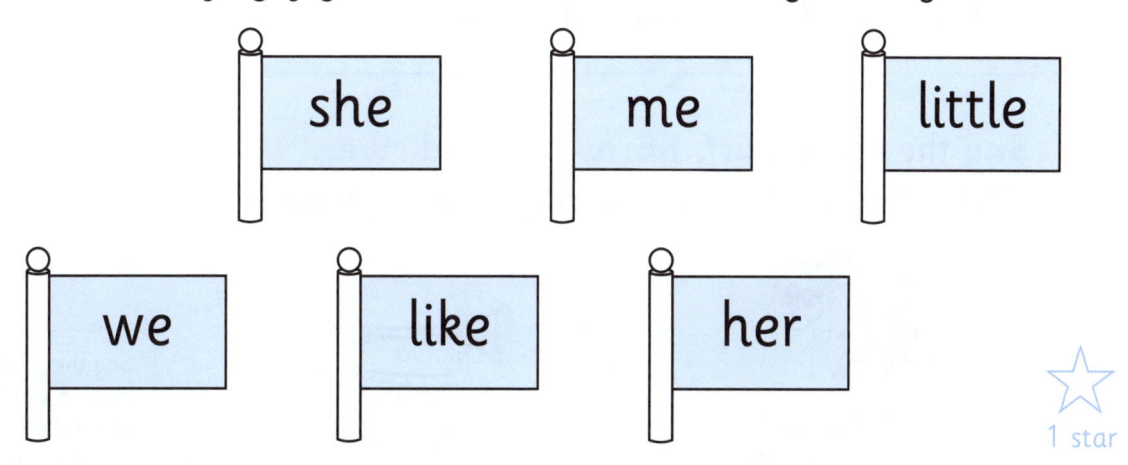

   she   me   little

   we   like   her

   1 star

5. The penguin is doing a trick and saying some tricky words.
   Listen to the tricky words. **Write** one word on each iceberg.

   they, you, my

   Score   stars

   1 star

Summer Term: Workout 9

Summer Term: Workout 10

Warm Up

1. **Look** at each card. **Say** the sound. **Copy** the letters.

| ur | or | ar | er |

1 star

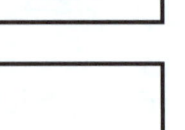

2. **Say** the words **surf**, **horn**, **star** and **river**.
   Write the words in the word frames by yourself.

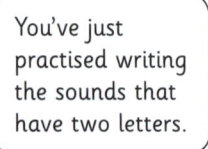

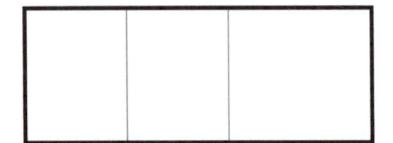

Say the sounds in each word. Write the letters.

You've just practised writing the sounds that have two letters.

1 star

3. **Look** at the picture. **Read** the captions.
   Circle the best caption for the picture.

   a dark curl

   a winter sport

   1 star

4. **Read** the tricky words on the flags.
   Circle the flag if you can read the word straight away.

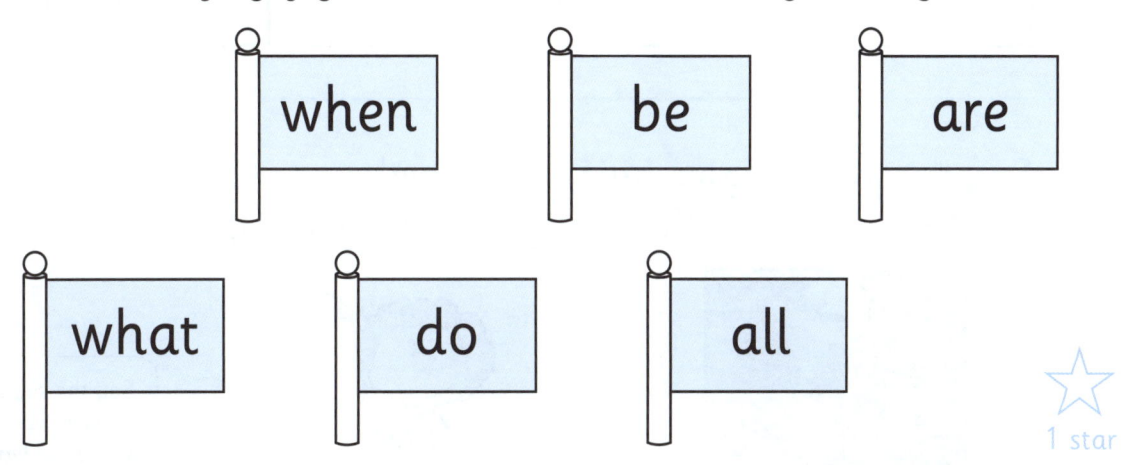

   when   be   are

   what   do   all

   1 star

5. The penguin is doing a trick and saying some tricky words.
   Listen to the tricky words. **Write** one word on each iceberg.

   was, he, me, we

   1 star

   Score   stars

   Summer Term: Workout 10

Summer Term: Workout 11

Warm Up

1. **Look** at each card. **Say** the sound. **Copy** the letters.

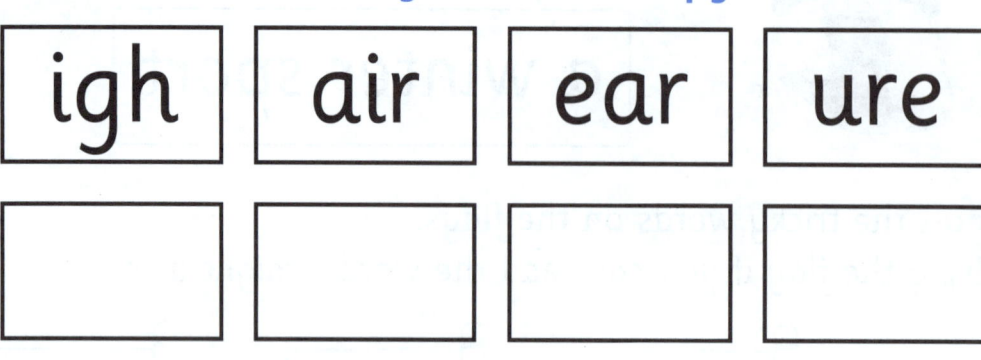

   | igh | air | ear | ure |

   1 star

2. **Say** the words **night**, **hair**, **spear** and **cure**.
   Write the words in the word frames by yourself.

   Say the sounds in each word. Write the letters.

   Each of these words has a sound that has three letters. Write all the letters in one box.

   1 star

3. **Look** at the picture. **Read** the captions.
   Circle the best caption for the picture.

   clear up manure

   repair a light

   1 star

4. **Read** the tricky words on the flags.
   Circle the flag if you can read the word straight away.

   I   some   were

   there   said   no

   1 star

5. The penguin is doing a trick and saying some tricky words.
   Listen to the tricky words. **Write** one word on each iceberg.

   (she, her, all)

   Score ☆☆☆☆☆ stars

   1 star

Summer Term: Workout 11

Summer Term: Workout 12

Warm Up

1. **Look** at each card. **Say** the sound. **Copy** the letters.

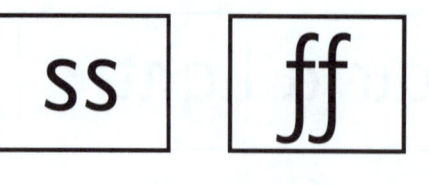

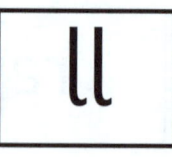

   | ss | ff | ll | zz |

   1 star

2. **Say** the words **dress**, **cuff**, **shell** and **fizz**.
   Write the words in the word frames by yourself.

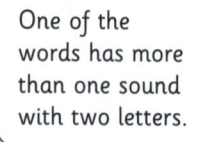

   One of the words has more than one sound with two letters.

   You've already practised one of the sounds earlier in the book.

   1 star

Summer Term: Workout 12   © CGP — not to be photocopied

3. **Look** at the picture. **Read** the captions.
   Circle the best caption for the picture.

   a jazz man puffs

   a duchess yells

   1 star

4. **Read** the question. **Circle** the correct answer.

   What is in a balloon?

   coffee   air

   1 star

5. The penguin is doing a trick and saying some tricky words.
   Listen to the tricky words. **Write** one word on each iceberg.

   be, are, no, I

   Score   stars

   1 star

© CGP — not to be photocopied

73

Summer Term: Workout 12

Progress Chart — Autumn Term

Fill in the progress chart after you finish each workout.

Put your scores in here to see how you've done.

	Score (out of five)
Workout 1	
Workout 2	
Workout 3	
Workout 4	
Workout 5	
Workout 6	
Workout 7	
Workout 8	
Workout 9	
Workout 10	
Workout 11	
Workout 12	

Progress Chart — Spring Term

Fill in the progress chart after you finish each workout.

Put your scores in here to see how you've done.

	Score (out of five)
Workout 1	
Workout 2	
Workout 3	
Workout 4	
Workout 5	
Workout 6	
Workout 7	
Workout 8	
Workout 9	
Workout 10	
Workout 11	
Workout 12	

Progress Chart — Summer Term

Fill in the progress chart after you finish each workout.

Put your scores in here to see how you've done.

	Score (out of five)
Workout 1	
Workout 2	
Workout 3	
Workout 4	
Workout 5	
Workout 6	
Workout 7	
Workout 8	
Workout 9	
Workout 10	
Workout 11	
Workout 12	